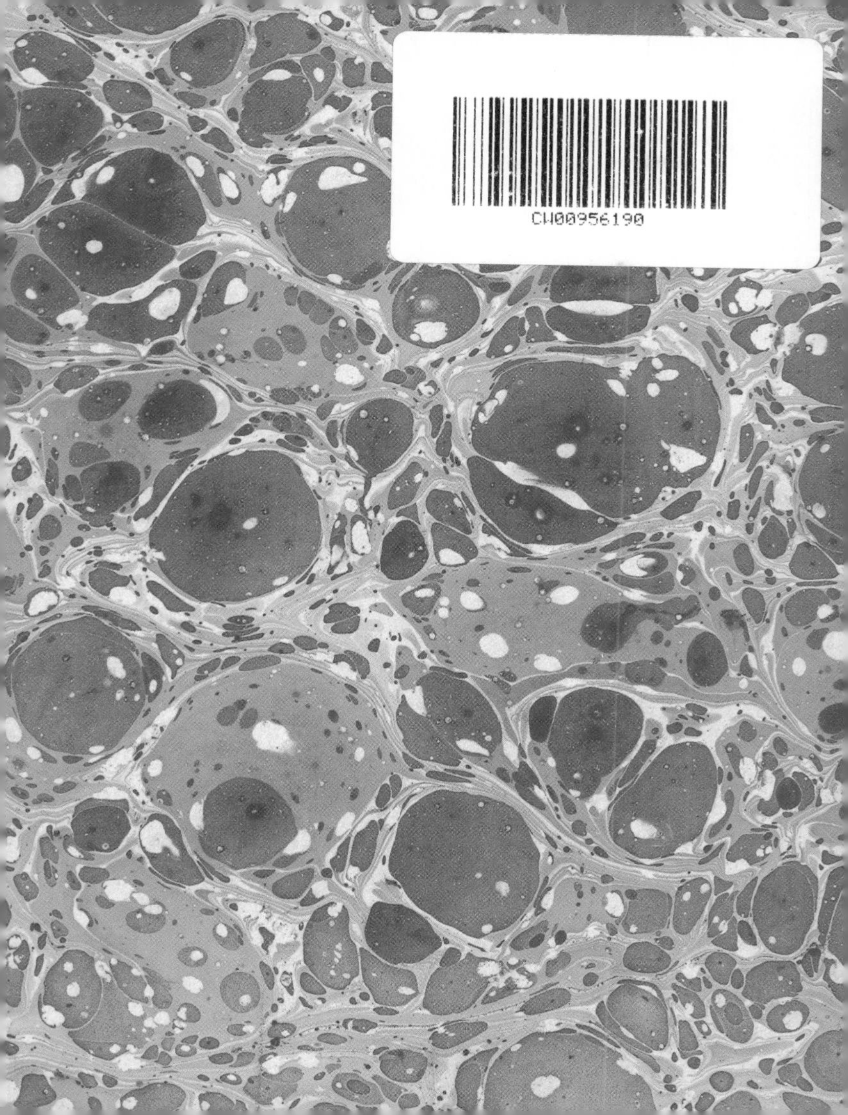
CW00956190

HONEY

JILL NORMAN

DORLING KINDERSLEY
LONDON

A DORLING KINDERSLEY BOOK

EDITOR LAURA HARPER

SENIOR EDITOR CAROLYN RYDEN

DESIGN MATHEWSON BULL

PHOTOGRAPHER DAVE KING

FIRST PUBLISHED IN GREAT BRITAIN IN 1990 BY
DORLING KINDERSLEY LIMITED
9 HENRIETTA STREET, LONDON WC2E 8PS

BRITISH LIBRARY CATALOGUING IN PUBLICATION DATA

NORMAN, JILL
HONEY
I. HONEY
I. TITLE II. SERIES
641·38

ISBN 0-86318-490-1

PRINTED AND BOUND IN HONG KONG
BY IMAGO

CONTENTS

INTRODUCTION

THE WORD 'HONEY' *comes from the Germanic root* hunaga, *meaning golden. For tens of thousands of years honey was almost the only available source of sugar in the countries where it was used – the universal sweetener. Ancient civilizations looked on the making of honey as a miracle, and even today, after much scientific research, honey remains something of a mystery – we still do not know everything about its constituents.*

Honey is made from the nectar which honeybees collect from flowers. Nectar itself is a sweet liquid produced by flowering plants to attract insects helpful in pollination. Honey contains much less moisture than the original nectar. About 80 percent of honey is sugar, mostly fructose and glucose. Sucrose, maltose and other more complex sugars are present in varying amounts, as are plant acids, mineral salts and a host of other substances – as many as 181 in all.

Honeycomb with honey

French honey label, c. 1940

French thread box label, c. 1900

When judging honey, there are three factors to consider – aroma and flavour, colour, and body. Aroma and flavour are influenced by the flowers from which the nectar is gathered. Colour can also be attributed to the flower and varies from white to very dark. Body depends on the skill with which honey is extracted from the comb and blended; if care is not taken at this stage, the honey may be too thin.

Acacia honey from southeast Europe is water-white and has a sweet, perfumed taste; clover, a major honey crop in many countries, produces greenish-white honey with a delicate aroma and flavour. Orange blossom honey – from Spain and Israel – is creamy white, with a fine, clear taste, as is lavender honey from Provence. Around the Mediterranean, rosemary yields a highly aromatic, granular, light amber honey, and classically renowned Greek thyme honey has an intense aroma, a rich flavour and a golden amber colour.

HONEY-GATHERING INSECTS

BY FAR THE MOST *important honey-producer is the common honeybee,* Apis mellifera, *native to the temperate and sub-tropical zones of Europe, Africa and the Middle East. Other species of honeybee native to Asia differ from* A. mellifera *in that they build their combs in the open. It is precisely* A. mellifera*'s habit of nesting in dark, enclosed spaces such as hollow trees and rock crevices that made it possible to transfer the bee to man-made hives in order to gain some control over its honey production.*

Worker bee

From a 16th-century manuscript

Bees at work on a honeycomb

All the various *Apis* species are 'social' insects that live in large and well-organized colonies, producing food both for immediate use and to store against the lean months of winter. It is these stores that attract predators, chief of which, of course, is man.

The honeybee gathers nectar with its tongue and carries it in a 'honey stomach' to the hive or nest. There, the nectar is passed to worker bees, who prepare it for storing by adding enzymes. As the worker bees transfer the nectar to a wax storage chamber, water is evaporated away, and it is this process, combined with the enzyme activity, that turns the nectar into honey.

HONEY FROM THE WILD

ALTHOUGH HONEY *was known and used long before recorded history, its real origin and composition were a mystery. 'Honey falls from the air, principally at the rising of the stars' wrote Aristotle in the 4th century BC. Much earlier, in Egypt, it was thought to stem from the tears of the god Re. Bees did no more than gather the 'honey-dew' clinging to plants. Bees and honey alike were venerated. Baby Zeus, hidden in a cave from his ravaging father, Time, was fed on milk and honey.*

Originally honey was 'hunted' from the nests of wild bees. In Spain, southern Africa and central India, prehistoric rock paintings show man gathering honey from combs hanging at dizzy heights, or from hollow trees and rocks.

Even today, much of India's honey is gathered from *Apis dorsata* nests in trees, and the honey-hunters of Tibet and Nepal are famous for their daring descents into ravines down ropes with nothing but a smoking torch for protection.

Spanish cave painting of a bee hunter

Poster from International Health Exhibition 1884

Bowl of honey with mixed flowers

HONEY FROM THE HIVE

THE EARLIEST RECORD *of keeping bees in hives was found in the sun temple erected* c. *2400BC by Ne-user-re at Sakhara near Cairo. The museum at Dokki displays two pots from a thousand years later that still contain honey. Beekeeping, as opposed to 'hunting' from nests, probably began at different times in different parts of the world.*

Egyptian hives were of the now familiar straw skep shape – a shape probably dictated by that of the swarm to be captured. Elsewhere in the Middle East hives were more often tubes of sun-burnt mud, arranged horizontally in stacks. Mud, pottery, wood and natural objects from logs to gourds are still used as hives in many parts of the world.

In northern Europe, where bees nested in hollow trees in vast forests, bee 'hunting' continued for much longer than around the Mediterranean. Nests were generally more accessible than those found in rock crevices in southern countries. As a result, a form of beekeeping developed whereby a keeper owned bee colonies in the trees. The practice spread across the

16th-century beekeepers

continent. Eventually men fixed hollow logs in the trees instead, and later similar logs were used upright on the ground.

In Britain, bees were certainly kept during the Bronze Age, when the wax was essential to the then prevalent method of bronze casting. Wax for candles and tapers long remained the most important product from the hive. In medieval times skeps were widely used, then upright wicker models, but hives were not much improved upon until wooden ones were introduced in the 17th century, influenced by advances in cabinet-making. These soon became the most popular type.

The mysterious activity in the bee colony prompted man to make hives in which the bees could be observed. In the 1830s Thomas Nutt – an apiarist – built some surprisingly complex ones, which had turrets and glass domes.

Despite beekeeping's ancient history, it was not until the 1800s that honey production became a serious industry, when a number of improvements at last paved the way for mechanization.

Beekeeper with straw skeps, c. 1910

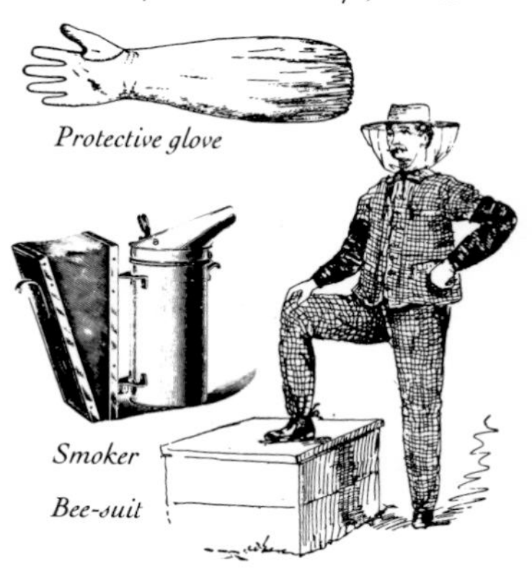

Protective glove

Smoker

Bee-suit

19th-century beekeeping equipment

HONEY FROM THE FARM

TRADITIONAL BEEKEEPING *meant that the whole comb was removed, pressed, heated and used up – and the bees, left without food supplies, starved or were killed. In 1852 an American vicar, The Rev. L. L. Langstroth, perfected a wooden hive based on the simple principle of surrounding movable frames with a 'bee space' – an area just large enough to discourage the bees from gluing their comb solidly to the wall of the hive.*

An officer in the Italian army, one Major Hruschka, then devised a way of extracting honey from the framed comb by centrifugal force – quick, clean, without heat (which can alter the colour and flavour of honey), and leaving the comb intact for the bees to use again. Present-day small honey extractors hold nine frames at a time and rotate them mechanically.

Honeycomb in its frame

The next step was to present the bees with an artificial foundation for the comb, thus reducing their labour and improving the reliability of the comb's shape. In the 1800s the A.I. Root Company of Medina, Ohio, developed a roller-press for making foundation plates of wax, almost as thin as the natural ones. This invention overcame the final obstacle on the way to large-scale honey production.

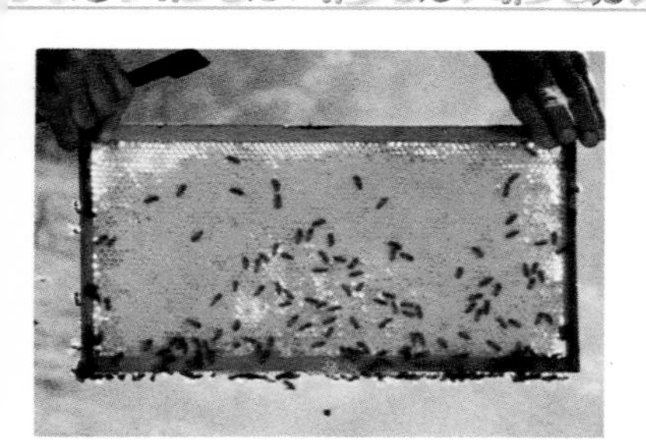

Honeycomb lifted from the hive

The different parts of a beehive

Honeycomb box

19th-century roller-press

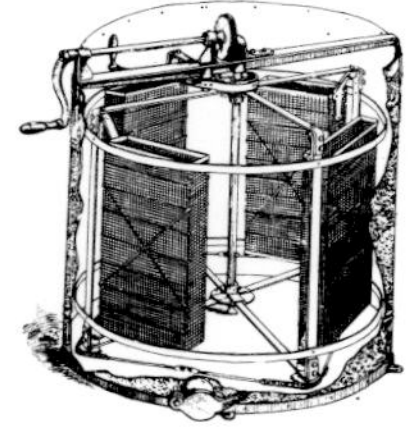

19th-century honey extractor

HONEY OFF THE SHELF

CURRENT WORLD PRODUCTION *of honey stands at about a million tons a year. The main producers are the USSR, China, the United States, Mexico, Canada and Argentina.*

Attempts at manufacturing honey artificially have so far proved unsuccessful. Adulteration has also been tried, mostly with sugar solutions – none are convincing, and most are easy to detect.

Most commercial honey is produced from nectar gathered from a variety of flowers. Single flower honey is readily available, although it costs more because it is harder to produce. Honey varies according to its geographical origin. It may be a blend from different countries, or the product of one specific country or region. The latter is usually more expensive than a blend.

Set honeys

The non-sugar solids in honey determine its colour, while the balance of sugars determines the texture – whether a honey is clear (liquid) or set (crystallized). The degree of crystallization is the only difference between the two. Most liquid honeys become granular when exposed to light or cold for some time. This does not affect their quality, and gentle heating (as in a moderately hot water bath) will usually restore liquidity.

Liquid honeys

FLOWER HONEY

THE FLAVOUR *of honey is closely related to its aroma. Some honeys, such as heather, are so pungent that they dominate all others. A beekeeper who produces single flower honeys must site his hives carefully and may have a low yield. In regions of mixed agriculture, crops such as rape and mustard contribute to mixed flower honeys and make it hard to detect specific flavours.*

Clover honey

Heather honey

Wild flower honey
Posy of wild flowers
Posy of mixed flowers
Mixed flower honey

HERB HONEY

*'T*HYME YIELDS HONEY *with the best flavour; the next best are Greek savory, wild thyme and marjoram. In the third class, but still of high quality, are rosemary and our Italian savory.'*

On Agriculture, *Columella, 1st century AD*

Today honeybees forage from many more herb flowers, particularly in the Mediterranean region where the fragrance of the herbs is heightened by the hot sun.

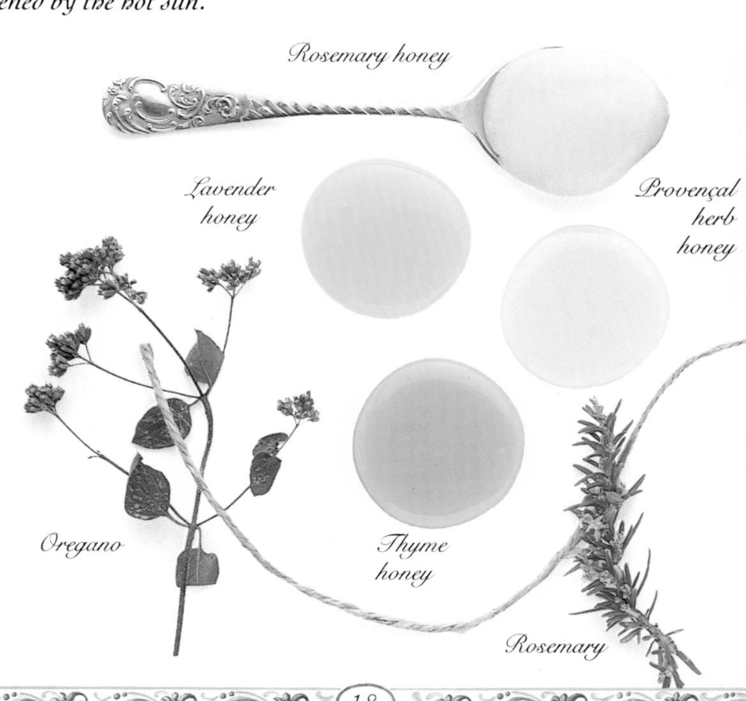

Posy of mixed herbs

HONEY FROM TREES

HIVES ARE OFTEN *placed within tracts of one tree variety during the flowering season; acacia in Hungary, lime in Poland, orange blossom in Spain, eucalyptus in Australia. Fruit trees are also a source of nectar in many countries.*

Orange blossom honey

Acacia honey

Apple blossom honey
Eucalyptus honey
Fir tree honey

HONEY IN BAKING & CONFECTIONERY

*H*ONEY WAS THE PRINCIPAL FORM *of sweetening until sugar cane reached Europe from the Middle East with the spread of Islam in the 9th century. Even then sugar remained a luxury until the 17th century, when it was widely planted in the New World. Today, despite the worldwide popularity of sugar, honey remains an essential ingredient in many delicacies.*

In the Middle East honey is used lavishly in confectionery, and sprinkled over pastries. The Greeks stir it into their thick, rich yogurt. Around the Mediterranean honey and nut confections are popular; halva, made with honey, nuts and sesame seeds, is a delicious sweet from the eastern Mediterranean; further west nougat comes into its own. It may be in the form of whole almonds and honey cooked together and pressed between sheets of rice paper as in Provence; a soft, marzipan-like *turrón de Jijona* from Spain; or the crisp Italian variety, made with honey, nuts, candied peel and egg white.

The countries north of the Alps invented a variety of honey biscuits made in shallow carved wooden moulds – the *Leckerli* and *Lebkuchen* of Switzerland and southern Germany, ginger biscuits and gingerbread of England. French *pain d'épices* is made from a more bread-like flour and honey dough, and Holland produces honey cakes, often containing chopped preserved ginger or candied sugar. In Scandinavia the flavourings are more likely to be cinnamon or cardamom and candied orange peel.

Halva

Leckerli

Italian advertisement for honey and honey sweets, c. 1949

Nougat with cherries and nuts

Nougat with almonds

Baked goods made with honey keep better and remain moist longer than those made with sugar. When replacing sugar with honey in a recipe, remember that honey is much sweeter, so replacing only half the sugar may be more to your taste. For example, where 4 oz of sugar is specified, use 2 oz of honey and 2 oz of sugar instead. Also honey has nearly 20 percent water, so add rather less liquid than asked for.

Recipes

All the recipes will serve 4, but some (such as cakes and pastries) will serve more

DUTCH HONEYCAKE

8 oz/250 g butter
5 eggs, separated
8 oz/250 g plain flour
1 teaspoon baking powder
6 oz/175 g liquid honey
2 tablespoons ginger syrup
6 pieces preserved ginger, chopped

Beat the butter to soften it, then beat in the egg yolks, one at a time. Sift the flour and baking powder together and add small amounts to the butter and egg mixture, alternating with the honey and syrup.

Stir in the ginger.

Whisk the egg whites until they stand in peaks and fold them in. Pour the mixture into a buttered 2 lb/1 kg loaf tin and bake in a preheated oven, 160°C/325°F/ gas 3, for 50–60 minutes. When ready it should be a light golden brown and be shrinking from the sides of the tin.

Cool on a rack.

This cake will keep for a week or more and is good spread with butter or honey.

Honey and Spice Cake

1 lb/500 g honey
4 oz/125 g butter
4 oz/125 g soft brown sugar
1 teaspoon ground cinnamon
1/2 teaspoon ground coriander
1/2 teaspoon ground cloves
4 eggs
1 lb/500 g plain flour
1 teaspoon baking powder
1 teaspoon baking soda
1 tablespoon milk
3 oz/75 g chopped walnuts
3 oz/75 g candied orange peel, chopped

Heat together gently the honey, butter and sugar. When the sugar has dissolved and the mixture is well blended, remove from the heat and stir in the spices. Leave to cool a little, then beat in the eggs, one at a time. Sift the flour and baking powder together. Dissolve the baking soda in the milk. Combine the flour and honey mixtures, beating well until smooth. Stir in the baking soda and milk. Add the nuts and peel, making sure they are well distributed throughout the batter. Grease a large loaf tin or a 10 in/25 cm round cake tin, dust well with flour, and shake out the excess. Pour in the batter and bake in a preheated oven, 180°C/350°F/gas 4, for 1 hour, or until a skewer inserted into the cake comes out clean. Cool in the tin on a wire rack.

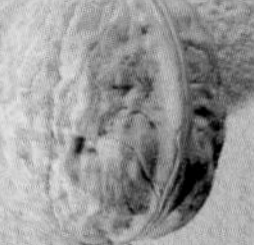

SPICED BISCUITS

6 oz/175 g butter
5 oz/150 g honey
grated zest of 2 lemons
3 eggs
12 oz/375 g plain flour
1 teaspoon baking powder
½ teaspoon ground mace
1 teaspoon ground cloves
2 teaspoons ground cinnamon
8 oz/250 g sugar

Melt the butter with the honey in a large pan. Add the lemon zest, put to one side and leave to cool. Whisk in the eggs, one at a time. Mix all the dry ingredients together in a separate bowl and add to the butter and honey, stirring well to blend. Cover the bowl with clingfilm and chill for 2 hours.

Drop teaspoons of the mixture onto buttered and floured baking sheets and bake in a preheated oven, 200°C/400°F/gas 6, for 10 minutes. Cool on a rack.

LECKERLI

Biscuits and cakes made with honey and spices are common throughout central and eastern Europe. They are often made for special occasions like Christmas or the feast of St Nicholas or Jewish new year. If stored in an airtight tin, they will mature and keep for a few weeks. This recipe comes from Switzerland.

1 lb/500 g plain flour
1 teaspoon baking powder
5 oz/150 g unblanched almonds, ground
6 oz/175 g sugar
½ teaspoon ground cloves
¾ teaspoon ground cinnamon
a grating of nutmeg
2 oz/50 g candied peel, chopped finely
2 tablespoons kirsch
6 oz/175 g honey

Mix together the flour, baking powder, almonds, sugar, spices and candied peel, and make a well in the centre. Heat the honey until just warm and pour it into the flour with the kirsch. Mix well to obtain a smooth dough.

Roll out on a floured surface to ¼ in/5 mm thick, cut into squares or diamonds and transfer to buttered and floured baking sheets. Bake in a preheated oven, 160°C/325°F/ gas 3, for about 15 minutes. If you wish, the warm leckerli can be brushed with a glaze made from 3 oz/75 g sugar boiled in 3 tablespoons water.

GREEK CREAM CHEESE AND HONEY PIE

4 oz/125 g plain flour
salt
1 tablespoon caster sugar
2 oz/50 g chilled butter
2 tablespoons iced water
8 oz/250 g ricotta
1/4 pint/150 ml double cream
3 tablespoons caster sugar
3 oz/75 g honey
1 teaspoon grated lemon zest
1 teaspoon ground cinnamon
3 eggs

Sift the flour with a pinch of salt, add the sugar and rub in the butter to obtain a breadcrumb texture. Add enough water to form the dough into a ball. Work it briefly with the heel of your hand, then wrap it in clingfilm and chill for 30 minutes. After chilling, roll out the pastry and line an 8 in/20 cm tart tin with a removable base. Beat the ricotta and cream together until smooth, then add the sugar, honey, lemon zest and cinnamon. Whisk the eggs lightly and stir them in, a little at a time. Pour the filling into the pastry shell, put the tin on a baking sheet and bake in a preheated oven, 180°C/350°F/gas 4, for 40–50 minutes. The pie can be eaten hot while it is puffed up and light, or cold when the consistency is more like that of cheesecake.

Briouats

These small Moroccan pastries filled with almond paste are soaked in honey.

12 oz/375 g almonds, blanched
4 tablespoons caster sugar
1 teaspoon ground cinnamon
4–5 tablespoons orange flower water
4 oz/125 g butter, melted
8 oz/250 g filo pastry
1 lb/500 g dark honey

Grind the almonds in a processor, adding the sugar when they are nearly smooth. Sprinkle in the cinnamon and add 1–2 tablespoons of the orange flower water and the same amount of the melted butter. Work to a paste.

Take the filo sheets one at a time, keeping the others covered to prevent them drying out. Brush the sheet with melted butter, cut it into 2 or 3 narrow strips and put a teaspoon of the almond paste near the end of each strip. Fold the corner over the filling to make a triangular shape. Flip the triangle over onto the next part of the filo strip, and continue in this way until you reach the end of the strip and have a triangular parcel. Press the edges closed. When all the pastries are made, bake them in a preheated oven, 160°C/325°F/gas 3, for 30 minutes.

Heat the honey with the remaining orange flower water, dip in the briouats for 3–4 minutes, then lift out and leave to dry. Serve cold.

ENGADIN NUT TORTE

A traditional recipe from the Engadin region of Switzerland.

8 oz/250 g plain flour
2 tablespoons caster sugar
salt
5 oz/150 g butter
1 egg
3–4 tablespoons iced water
1 oz/25 g butter
8 oz/250 g hazelnuts, chopped coarsely
2 oz/50 g almonds, chopped coarsely
6 oz/175 g sugar
3/4 pint/450 ml double cream
4 tablespoons honey
1 egg yolk

Make the pastry as described on p.28, using the egg and enough water to form the dough into a ball.

Melt 1 oz/25 g butter in a heavy pan and brown the nuts for a few minutes, then stir in the sugar, and when it has melted, the cream. Stir well to blend in the cream and then add the honey.

Roll out two-thirds of the pastry to line a 9 in/23 cm loose bottomed cake tin, to a height of about 2 in/5 cm. Pour in the filling and fold the edges of the pastry down over it. Wet the pastry edge lightly and cover the torte with a lid made from the remaining pastry. Press the edges together. Prick all over with a fork and brush with egg yolk. Bake in a preheated oven, 180°C/350°F/gas 4, for 50–60 minutes. If the top starts to colour too much, cover it with foil. Serve cold.

*P*ANCAKES WITH HONEY

7 oz/200 g plain flour
salt
2 eggs
3/4 pint/450 ml milk
4 oz/125 g butter
6 oz/175 g liquid honey

Sift the flour into a bowl with a pinch of salt. Make a well in the centre and add the eggs, one at a time, beating well. Pour the milk in slowly, still beating, until you have a fairly thick, smooth batter. Melt half the butter and stir it in. Leave the batter to rest for at least an hour. Just before frying the pancakes, heat the honey gently and keep it warm. Melt a small piece of butter in a frying pan, pour in a ladle of batter, tilt the pan to spread it evenly and cook for about 2 minutes, until the underside is golden brown. Turn with a spatula and cook the other side. Slide the pancake onto a plate and brush with warm honey. Roll the pancake up and transfer to a serving dish in a warm oven while making the rest of the pancakes. Serve more warmed honey with them if you wish.

*W*INTER FRUIT SALAD

8 oz/250 g dried apricots
3 oz/75 g sultanas
4 oz/125 g almonds, blanched
2 oz/50 g pistachios
3 tablespoons honey
2 tablespoons rose water
2 bananas
a grating of nutmeg

Put the dried fruits and nuts in a bowl, spoon over the honey and rose water and add just enough water to cover. Leave to soak for 24 hours. Slice the bananas and stir them into the fruit salad, making sure they are covered by the liquid. Add a little grated nutmeg and leave for a further 3–4 hours before serving.

Honey Ice Cream

1/2 pint/300 ml milk
5 oz/150 g wild flower honey
3 egg yolks
3 tablespoons poppy seeds (optional)
1/4 pint/150 ml double cream

Bring the milk to the boil, then stir in the honey. Whisk the egg yolks until pale, pour over a little of the milk, whisk well and pour the egg mixture into the pan. Return it to a low heat and cook gently until the mixture coats the back of a spoon. Stir in the poppy seeds, if you are using them, and leave to cool. Whip the cream lightly, fold it into the custard and freeze in an ice cream machine.

Amaretti Ice Cream

3/4 pint/450 ml double cream
2–3 tablespoons liquid honey
6 amaretti, crushed
3 tablespoons amaretti liqueur or cognac

Whisk the cream with the honey until it starts to thicken, then freeze it in a tray until the bottom and sides are firm. Turn the cream out into a chilled bowl, beat it for a minute or two, then stir in the amaretti and the liqueur. Pour it back into the tray and freeze until set.

Orange Compote

6 large oranges
6 oz/175 g sugar
6 oz/175 g honey
5 tablespoons water
5 tablespoons sherry
1 stick cinnamon

Remove all the peel and membrane from the oranges and break carefully into segments. Put all the remaining ingredients in a heavy pan and bring slowly to the boil. Boil for 5 minutes until you have a thick syrup. Add the orange segments to the syrup, heat through for 2–3 minutes, then turn the oranges and syrup into a serving dish. Remove the cinnamon and serve very cold.

*P*EARS IN HONEY

4 pears
4 tablespoons honey
½ pint/300 ml water
2 tablespoons lemon juice
1 vanilla pod
2 tablespoons chopped pistachio nuts
whipped cream

Peel the pears, cut them in half and remove the cores. Bring the honey, water, lemon juice and vanilla pod to the boil and pour the syrup over the pears in a small pan. Cover and simmer until the pears are cooked, basting them from time to time with the syrup if necessary. Remove the vanilla pod and transfer the pears to a serving dish. Sprinkle with the pistachios and serve cold with whipped cream.

QUINCE PRESERVE

3 lb/1.5 kg quinces
juice of 1 lemon
1 lb/500 g sugar
8 oz/250 g honey
1 stick cinnamon

Wipe the quinces to remove the fuzz and peel them thinly, keeping the skins. Grate the flesh coarsely and put it in a bowl with the lemon juice and half the sugar. Mix well.

Put the skins and cores in a pan, cover with cold water and boil for 30 minutes. Drain and measure 1 pint/600 ml of the liquid, making up the amount with water if necessary. Add the remaining sugar, the honey and cinnamon to the liquid and bring to the boil slowly, stirring to dissolve the sugar. Boil for 3–4 minutes, then cool.

Add the grated quince to the syrup, bring to a simmer and simmer for about 1 hour, stirring frequently as the preserve thickens. It is ready when it forms a thick flake on a wooden spoon. Leave to cool before potting in sterilized jars.

ATHOLE BROSE

An old Scottish beverage, this version comes from *The Cook and Housewife's Manual*, 1833, by Meg Dods.

'Mix with *a cupful of heather honey, two cupfuls of whisky*, alias mountain dew; *brandy* and *rum* are also used, though the combination they form with honey cannot be called Athole Brose.'

A more recent recipe from F. Marian McNeill is as follows:

Beat *1½ cups double cream* to a froth and stir in *1 cup of lightly toasted oatmeal* and *½ cup of heather honey*. Just before serving, stir in *2 glasses of whisky*.

ONION CONFIT

4 oz/125 g butter
1 lb/500 g onions, sliced finely
salt and pepper
1/2 teaspoon ground coriander
3 tablespoons honey
3 tablespoons sherry vinegar

Melt the butter and when it is a deep golden colour put in the onions. Season with salt, pepper and coriander. Cover the pan and cook on the lowest possible heat for 30 minutes, stirring from time to time. Add the honey and vinegar and cook for another 30–45 minutes until the onions are very soft. Leave uncovered for the last 15 minutes to thicken the confit.

BAKED PARSNIPS

1 lb/500 g parsnips
salt and pepper
a pinch of ground ginger
2 oz/50 g butter
2 tablespoons pine nuts
1 tablespoon honey
2 tablespoons whisky

Cut the parsnips in half lengthways and cook in boiling salted water until just tender. Drain and cut the pieces into 1/4 in/5 mm slices. Put them in one layer in a buttered baking dish and season with salt and pepper and a little ground ginger. Heat the butter and lightly fry the pine nuts, then stir in the honey and whisky. Blend well together and drizzle the sauce over the parsnips. Bake in a preheated oven, 180°C/350°F/ gas 4, for 10–12 minutes.

BAKED BEANS

12 oz/375 g haricot beans, soaked
1 large onion, sliced
2 cloves garlic, chopped
1 tablespoon Dijon mustard
4 tablespoons honey
salt and pepper
chopped parsley

Cook the beans in water until just soft – about 40 minutes. Drain, reserving the cooking liquid. Transfer them to a casserole and mix with the onion, garlic, mustard, honey and enough of the cooking liquid to prevent the beans becoming dry. Season with salt and pepper. Cover and bake in a preheated oven, 180°C/350°F/ gas 4, for 30 minutes. Check half way through the cooking time that the beans have not dried out, and add a little more water if necessary. Stir in the chopped parsley just before serving.

SWEET AND SOUR COURGETTES

1 lb/500 g courgettes
1 small onion, chopped
2 tablespoons oil
2 tablespoons lemon juice
1 tablespoon honey
salt and pepper
a handful of chopped parsley

Slice the courgettes fairly thinly. Sauté the onion in the oil until it starts to turn golden, then add the courgettes. Sauté for a few minutes, turning to allow the oil to coat all the courgettes, then cover the pan, lower the heat and cook for 5–6 minutes. Stir in the lemon juice and honey, and season with salt and pepper. Turn up the heat and cook uncovered until the courgettes are tender but not too soft and there is a small amount of syrupy glaze in the pan. Serve sprinkled with parsley.

SWEET AND SOUR BARBECUE SAUCE

1 clove garlic
1 teaspoon salt
1/2 teaspoon chilli powder
1/2 teaspoon mustard powder
2 tablespoons honey
3 tablespoons lemon juice
juice of 1 orange
3 tablespoons water

Crush the garlic with the salt, add the chilli and mustard powders, and then the liquid ingredients. Serve with barbecued chicken or pork.

MOROCCAN CARROT SALAD

1 lb/500 g carrots
1/2 teaspoon ground ginger
1/2 teaspoon ground cinnamon
1/2 teaspoon paprika
1 tablespoon honey
juice of 1 lemon
2 tablespoons olive oil
salt
1/2 teaspoon caraway seeds

Boil the carrots until tender, then drain and dice. Make a dressing with the other ingredients and toss the carrots in it.

BARBECUE MARINADE

1 clove garlic, crushed
small piece of fresh ginger, sliced
4 tablespoons soy sauce
1 tablespoon honey
3 tablespoons dry sherry
a pinch of ground cloves
a pinch of ground allspice

Combine all the ingredients and use to marinate spare ribs, chicken or fish.

TWO GLAZES FOR GRILLED OR ROAST MEAT

2 tablespoons honey
2 tablespoons water
1 teaspoon five spice powder

Combine and use to glaze meat 5–10 minutes before the end of the cooking time.

2 tablespoons honey
1 tablespoon soy sauce
1 tablespoon lemon juice
1/2 teaspoon ground anise or cloves

Use as above.

PORK BRAISED WITH CIDER AND HONEY

2 oz/50 g butter
2 lb/1 kg pork loin, boned and rolled
4 shallots, chopped
4 tablespoons honey
1 strip lemon peel
1 strip orange peel
1/4 teaspoon ground cardamom
salt and pepper
1/2 pint/300 ml dry cider

Melt the butter in a casserole and brown the meat on all sides. Add the shallots, honey, lemon and orange peel and season with cardamom, salt and pepper. Pour over the cider and bring to the boil. Cover the casserole tightly and transfer it to a preheated oven, 180°C/350°F/gas 4, for about 1 1/2 hours. Lift out the meat and reduce the braising liquid to serve as a sauce.

LAMB TAGINE WITH HONEY

A rich spiced Moroccan stew.

2 lb/1 kg lean lamb, cubed
2 tablespoons oil
½ teaspoon ground ginger
½ teaspoon ground coriander
1 cinnamon stick
1 teaspoon ground black pepper
¼ teaspoon saffron threads
salt
4 onions
8 oz/250 g prunes, soaked (optional)
1 tablespoon chopped parsley
1 tablespoon chopped chervil
1 teaspoon ground cinnamon
2 tablespoons liquid honey

Put the lamb in a heavy casserole with the oil, spices (except the ground cinnamon), salt, and 2 onions, chopped finely. Add enough water just to cover the meat, bring to the boil, skim and then cover the pan and simmer very slowly for 1½–2 hours until the meat is tender.

Slice the remaining onions thinly and add them to the casserole with the drained prunes, if you are including them. Cook for 30 minutes. Stir in the herbs, ground cinnamon and honey, and cook for another 20–30 minutes. Remove the cinnamon stick and serve.

INDEX

ACKNOWLEDGEMENTS

The publishers would like to thank the following

· TYPESETTING ·
TRADESPOOLS LTD
FROME

PHOTOGRAPHIC
· ASSISTANCE ·
JONATHAN BUCKLEY

JACKET
· PHOTOGRAPHY ·
DAVE KING

· ILLUSTRATOR ·
JANE THOMSON

· REPRODUCTION ·
COLOURSCAN
SINGAPORE

The publishers would like to thank the following for permission to use photographs and objects

PAGE **5** RETROGRAPH ARCHIVE COLLECTION, LONDON PAGE **6** INTERNATIONAL BEE RESEARCH ASSOCIATION, CARDIFF PAGE **7** OXFORD SCIENTIFIC FILMS, OXFORD PAGE **8** INTERNATIONAL BEE RESEARCH ASSOCIATION, CARDIFF PAGE **9** ROBERT OPIE COLLECTION, LONDON PAGES **10-11** MARY EVANS PICTURE LIBRARY, LONDON PAGES **12-13** CENTRE, HONEYSUCKLE FOODS, OXFORD; TOP, THE AUSTRALIAN HONEY CORPORATION, LONDON PAGES **22-3** RETROGRAPH ARCHIVE COLLECTION, LONDON PAGE **33** ST PETER'S BROWSERY, LONDON PAGE **37** THOMAS GOODE & CO (LONDON) LTD

GWEN EDMONDS FOR ADDITIONAL HELP • MARION BURDENUIK FOR PREPARING FOOD
INTERNATIONAL BEE RESEARCH ASSOCIATION • GALES HONEY

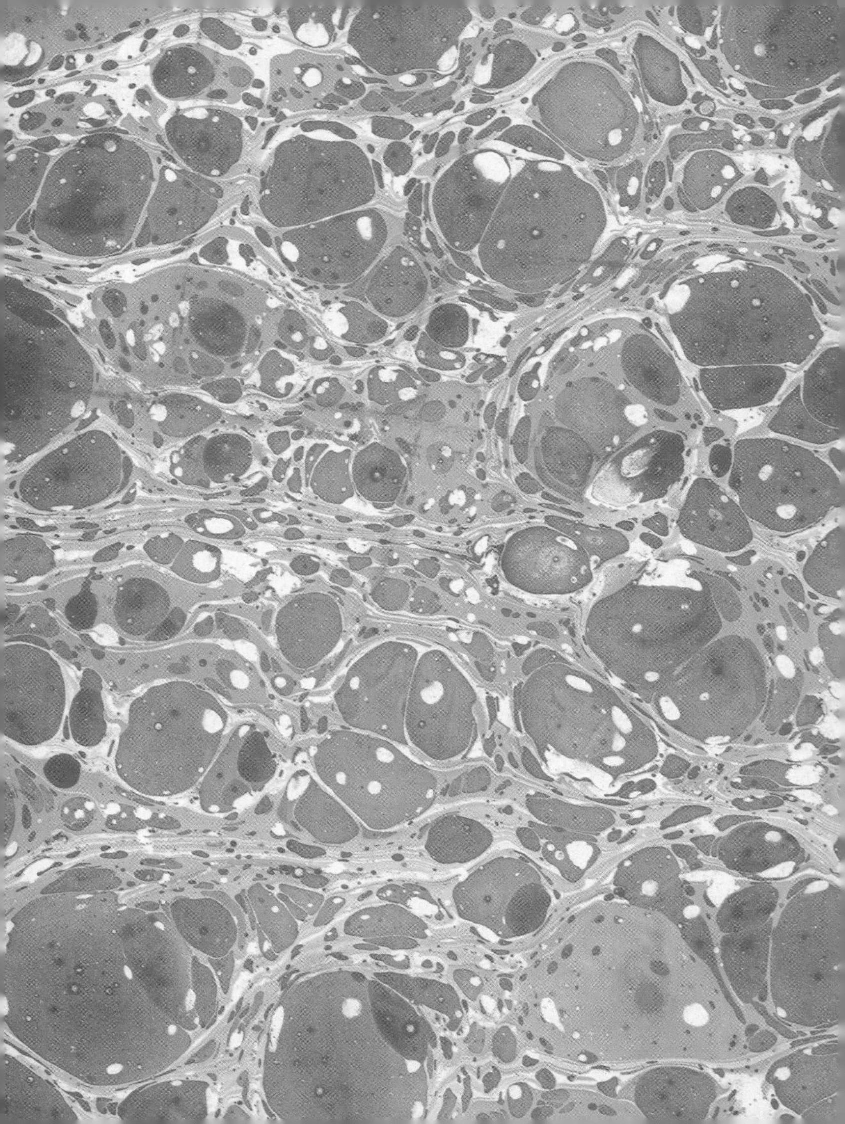